WHEN HER BAGGAGE WEIGHED NOTHING

KOJAK

 www.trafford.com

North America & international
toll-free: 844-688-6899 (USA & Canada)
fax: 812 355 4082

T his may not comply to all but it will resignate with most of you who left home or loss that love one that had us focus. When we began living freely on our own we began to stray I wanna pause using "we or us" I would love to share the first 20 years of my life I have absolutely no regrets looking back volunteering myself to what felt right to me in that moment fortunately I had the great experience of sharing life with my great great grandmother my mother mother's mother and as I said in the beginning this may resignate with most Sunday service was regular knowing its holy door was a mile and a half walking distance from the house 6-8 years 'ol I remember the preacher swallowed up in a gown saying these words to his congregation for I know the plans I have for you declares the Lord and I have to give the reverend his credit for delivering that message maybe its the one message that assured me that I was one day gonna be an adult 8 years old isn't an age that you remember alot but for some reason I can maybe because my moms and I went through it 8 years 'ol and at that age I was very small in statue and its an age where you definitely can feel defenseless and with my moms first marriage that was the case not only did that one thing happen I was too married into a family where I had to become a step brother nothing I asked for just had to live it. Could I have been physically abused as well sure, but I have no recollection of any of that taking place.

To hear your mother crying out loud from behind closed doors "Just does something to you" lets just say it boiled my blood and I kept quiet to not worsten the situation you can sit in front of a TV. and watch cartoon after cartoon and the same way you remember whats being said you'll always remember this "Kids put your coat and shoes on" and you knew then it was gonna be along night.

Back then you could run to someone's house for safety but it wasn't much done because no one wanted to interfere I went to school I acted out I was paddled by my uncle's friend who worked as a teacher and when I got home I'm pretty sure I was punished again the thought of this person belonging to someone else it never surface in their mind but when it came to my mother I knew she claimed me and would have did whatever to protect me as I stated before "Nothing physical happen to me."

You might ask yourself when she left why didn't she stay gone because the phrase was "Kids put on your coat and shoes" and it was no longer just me so yeah we returned alcohol and drugs haven't just appeared out of no where could it have been a factor it could've been I stayed mad at my biological dad for along time he up north and we down south he mad at her cause she left with me happy moments didn't make things better for me I was mad no one asking was we alright and no one did too much about the situation when it came to me there was so much I was thankful for because things could've been different but lets be honest I became bitter I now had to work on a attitude to make sure I wasn't looked at as a punk or someone that can be bullied so many years spent thriving for a happy marriage it ended she walked away "Walked not ran" so not all dignity wasn't loss because her and I we moved to Florida this time I'm a big brother I remember eating alot of restaurant and using those small bars of soap that hotels provided B. W. you guessed it she worked both we in Florida.

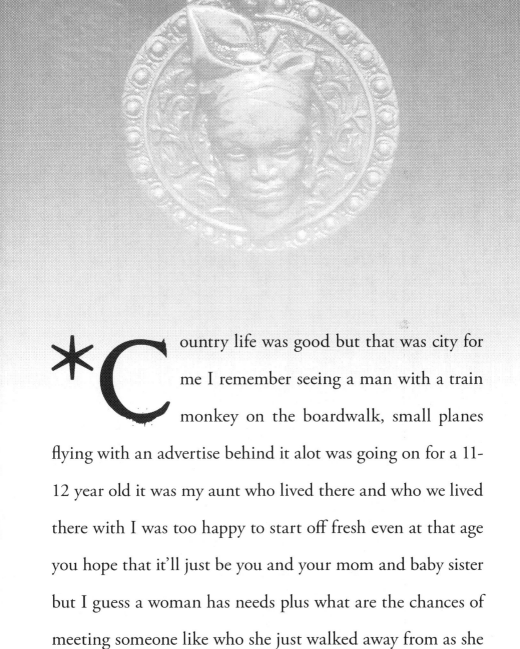

*Country life was good but that was city for me I remember seeing a man with a train monkey on the boardwalk, small planes flying with an advertise behind it alot was going on for a 11-12 year old it was my aunt who lived there and who we lived there with I was too happy to start off fresh even at that age you hope that it'll just be you and your mom and baby sister but I guess a woman has needs plus what are the chances of meeting someone like who she just walked away from as she worked two jobs to come into her own eventually she finally

5

did. If you the reader would allow me to give you 'alil bit of insight I stated we moved to Florida meaning up the street and around the corner wasn't gonna cut it she felt that we had to relocate and that meant planning and planning is a tool of domestic violence that will possibily save your life.

---

* I've always considered myself as a good natured person but what we went through did something to me what it did was changed my attitude because throughout life there will be things to make you worst or better at that age in my life it hadn't worsten me but I knew that was going to resurface throughout my life meanwhile living in Florida she met someone and if I just say well I be damn you already know what I'm talking about different guy same shit couple years later we whined up in Georgia for a second time and who would have thought my childhood would have come to an end.

* I began working with some out-of-towners bailing pinestraw and I learned to cook certain small meals and buy my lil sister school clothes all because my mother stayed in the hospital perhaps it was from the abuser or just being ill all I know is that I never stopped it later became a outlet for me to not be home and learn and even bring a little food home because I chose working restaurants for safety.

Georgia. was short lived we whined up in another city in Georgia. and if you're thinking a upstair downstair 2 car garage home wrong answer "they called it Tha' Bottom 2 apartment complexes side by side outside of that was a small blue building they sold pipes, baggies, scales, tapes etc.

Another familiar spot was tha' Market it sold small items such as can goods, tissue, tooth paste all the small things you may need and it had a dirt floor. There was a grocery store built that had two fried chicken restaurants around the corner was a small night club and behind the night club was a small wooded area and what I'm about to tell you is extremely important its how I became to be a small time local hustler by living in tha' country I had a good sense of smell and when it rained or the day was hot I was familiar with a smell... the smell of baits you heard right fishing baits under boards, plastic panels juicy ass nightcrawlers I had 3 buyers a heap of worms for $7.00 and I was the only one who knew bout the spot another thing that got my attention there was a green box on the corner of our apartment building and when I tell you it got hot it was hot hot enough to watch nightcrawlers wiggle like crazy as I placed them on it the baits were my hustle but my behavior was vindictive.

⋅⋅⋅◆◆◆◆⋅⋅⋅

* S. Supermarket had a aisle with small toys and for whatever reason I stole a pair of grey handcuffs with the key

luckily I didn't get the cops called on me I was banned from the store not realizing my mother was one day gonna send me for something.

Third grade, my teacher a very old lady she grew wise to my behavior shortly after that the permission note to paddle was send home it was signed and returned but I didn't sign it my mother did just for a moment allow me to bring you up to par" others seen me as a good natured boy but issues was starting to surface and the communication between my mother, the teacher, and the principal became one and I began wearing two pair of pants to school behavior had already set in.

--- ✦✦✦✦✦ ---

* This gesture was a helpful one but either I was gonna graduate or we were gonna move we moved right in the apartment complex next door it was very active cops chasing dealers one day I'm outside playing ran across somebody

stashspot a large bag of weed with brown envelopes inside luckily I didn't know anyone who smoked or I would have had a new hustle. I took it home to mama of course I was questioned where I got it and I explained I found it I stood right there in the bathroom and watch her flush it and I never mention it to no one.

———————————— ✦✦◆✦✦ ————————————

* Getting paddled did some justice I whined up at a Middle School in Georgia and yet I still managed to misbehave a couple of us we thought it was cool to remove emblems off of people cars but when word got 'round that the cops was asking questions I stopped and never did it again.

———————————— ✦✦◆✦✦ ————————————

* I was very adventurous I rode my bike all over the city but I always taught myself what side to look for sliding doors on

commercial vans and I always made it my business to avoid them.

After years in the projects we moved to 4th Street in the downtown area a pretty large duplex with a shared porch I remember going to this hotel that had fish in a 'lil man made stream I caught it took it home put it in the bath tub and shot it with a pellet gun that no one knew I had and I don't even know where I acquired it. My mom use to send me to the store for cigarettes and as soon as she have company it was the perfect time to ask to go outside and on the way out grab a couple of half smoked ones out the ashtray to see why she smoked them.

◆ ◆ ◆ ◆ ◆

* Alot of the time I ventured off on my bike 'til the street lights came on. It really wasn't much to do as a 13-14 yr. 'ol a recreation center was close so I'll go there and bet that no one could beat me in foose ball its call gambling now we

stayed at 4th Street for a good while and all the while she was doing it by herself until she met a guy who became her second husband and moved us to a place where my sister and I shared a room and the street was very high volume. I met friends and out of no where I met bullies what came with this second marriage his kids (2) that I wasn't thrill to share my time with but hey what could I do we spent lots of time at his mothers' house mainly all day you know what that do to a kid, it seemed things were re-occurring having to share what was mine. I'm now attending another Middle School and my attitude is flarring up I'm changing grades in the teacher book putting tacks in his wooden desk chair, twisting up paper to flick off my pencil and now I'm tested by another student we fought in the hall did I lose cause everyone said so or was I seeing if I was scared to O.K. give or take I lost the fight but proved my point. The neighborhood wasn't polite to me from somewhere I acquired an aluminum baseball bat and I was prepared to use it his kids didn't live with us from time to time I stayed somewhere I wasn't thrill about no one but my sister. It didn't matter.

——————————◆◆◆◆——————————

* Now don't think we lived somewhere for months we did years 3-4 tops along time to put up with bullshit from neighborhood kids after the move out, didn't matter where we were moving I was ready to walk back in at the end of the day neighborhood was quiet for the most part and the houses were well kept up I attended my third Middle School had a fairly good school year but back in the neighborhood right across the street from me lived a cute girl very light skin with thick black hair and she had the boys attention. I liked her too I'm in the front yard doing back flips cause the yard was slanted playing music by The Boys "Dial My Heart" hoping she would notice but there was one guy who made it known to me that he would fight me over her it was always unexpected drama in my path as we moved around

I rode my bike exploring more of the city at that age it was comfortable for me to run the street and not just be a home body wasn't it the reason she gave me a key.

---

* As I stated we lived places year 'round but this next move is where living-in-that moment just felt right we moved to another apartment where I attended my fourth Middle School and I have to admit I liked this one out of all the places we lived it was just in a good part of town things happen between adults this move was once again me my mother and my sister to give you a better understanding this apartment complex from a sky view was in the shape of a cent symbol with lots of apartment units, families and girls as I stated before its always something bout being the new kid.

I clearly remember my first day of school I had gym keep in mind I don't know anyone and know one knows me a young black male sitting at the top of the bleachers flat out says to me as I'm walking pass "You think you hard" and I proceed to find me a spot on the bleacher away from him cause that didn't seem like friendly talk and no nothing ever transpired between him and I but wait it get better this school was right next door to where we were living and after school I would go home and sit outside on the steps and just observed the neighborhood and the one thing I found out is that alot of the ones in the neighborhood didn't live in the complex they came from the hill a small neighborhood walking distance from where I lived what comes with an apartment complex with girls "show-offs" and I kept running into them. I had one guy tell me that he would kill me and we never once met but that was living in the moment where I would have had to take action if needed facing off with him and some others is how I met my bestfriend / my brother who clearly said oh yall ain't gon jump him and since that moment him and I we were inseparable and he introduce his self as Brian Broadnax and

15

we later gave him the nick name "Duck." Alot went on in the on going years I attended Westside High School and graduated and I worked and been working ever since I just wanna get back on the topic "When her baggage weighed nothing" she didn't always have the money but she managed every car that she owned wasn't the best liable transportation packing up an apartment to move is never fun but she my mother was all we had she would go-on to trust others I didn't. She putting up with crap at work and I'm putting up with fools in the neighborhood it was never a settle down moment I'm not gonna go any further bout me but every relationship that I got in wasn't a good one.

✦ ✦ ✦ ✦ ✦ ✦ ✦

* Emotional abuse is just as bad as physical abuse and plenty of times I had to step out of character using profanity calling whomever out their name or just being agitated the realist thing that I'll tell you is I was in my early 30's before I could

get comfortable enough to remove my shoes I stayed dressed and in the street all the time. When people show you who they are you take it in I'm giving myself room to grow as of now I won't make a good step brother thats a fact from life experiences but what I didn't realize they probably went through what I did but everyone came off angry there were days I literally fought my baby sister because of situations I didn't wanna experience I use to think that every woman driving with her kids was like us trying to get away from some one hurting them. It's one thing to dream a nightmare but to wake up living with a monster is baffling.

---

* For the longest time I felt like I was an attractive young man covering an attitude and thats how most of us are until it becomes to much.

Even though I questioned why God would even let that happen to my mother I still was thankful under His blessing that she didn't die on me. As I write this I realize how strong a woman has to be to tolerate and to stragergize what did not have to be I firmly believe that my mother would advise you to take nothing grab whats yours and breathing and seek shelter else where.

・◆◆◆◆・

* We all heard the saying a woman can't teach a boy to be a man well I beg the differ as my stomach grawled at times and how she would drive asking God to show her the way and to give her the answer on what to do next. No man abuses a woman just because that man had to have undealt with issues bottled up we come in all inticing forms tall, dark, handsome, and charming but its what you don't know that will one day be revealed as I addressed earlier verbal abuse is no better and every situation I ran into early in my life cause me to get out of character domestic violence is a

learned behavior and its zero to one hundred attitude takes over the aggressor.

—————⸱♦⸱♦⸱♦⸱—————

* The early 70's and 80's were hard on women and I'll gladly take the beating behind this handwritten self publish manuscript because cemetaries around the world holds the voices that second guessed if that would be the only time he say it'll happen. Abuse can start as early as 1 years old depends on the aggressor ever been picked up and tossed into a swimming pool at that age knowing you can't swim and you grow up afraid on being on boats and missing out on group trips such as cruises because that one incident struck fear in you.

I take it we all have alil abuser in us we send children to bed knowing that they at that age are afraid of the dark that may sound harmless but its a life long factor which builds fear in the child and fear is totally different from feeling loved and secured. I'm still trying to figure out what made man who suppose to be his soul mate protector why do we feel like threats and verbal and physical abuse is whats required to gain his respect was it the fact that the bible told us Eve got us banished from the Garden of Eden, was it the physical battle where Cain killed his brother Abel. I'm 46 years old and I'm still having trouble finding out why this act of violence has taking place and not only that has taking lives.

When I think back on why my mother dealt with her encounter for so long and just did not move on clearly she will say "I was young and in love but not giving herself time meaning a year or two of dating in that time frame would he have displayed that aggression or would he continue to wine and dine her for the appropriate love that she never got to endure. My mother in my eyes is one of the most beautifulliest woman I can claim that under no other circumstances belong to me so why would I want to see her with a black eye, a crocked or jammed finger from raising her hand out of protection.

Why would I want to see her missing a tooth or a broken arm or rib, burned, slapped, starved, or treated unfairly because one person can't wrap their mind around she will always belong to me.

As I write this I want the woman who has already experience this act of violence to stand strong pushing fear to the wayside I can't help but say this once again cemetaries around the world are packed with voices who second guessed if it would happen again domestic violence is an act of abuse that. Starts in the home children as young as infants get this backlash and whined up on ventilators and in the city protective care knowing what the chances are to place them into a loving home with stable thinking people each relationship that I gotten involved in definitely was a challenge knowing what I had already been through I couldn't resist the verbal abuse but I take the credit for ending it before it progressed leaving me to only be looked at as a monster when ever we were out in public.

----◆◆◆◆◆----

* My faith wasn't my focol point at that time because it was to easily to push my buttons and get that reaction that I'm askin' you to be aware of.

Making a way out of no way is impossible so I ask why would anyone wanna forcefully insinuate that as if its that easy.

At some point we all seem to let our temper flair but when objects get thrown and prepared meals get swipped off the table and onto the floor thats a sure sign of passive aggressive behavior not only have women been abused they have also been sodomized forcefully against her will leaving her confidence battered and her ego bruised when children witness this unstable act of violence within the home they quickly grasp the unorthodox behavior and takes it out on pets and younger siblings as if they are the aggressor. Its already a task trying to treat a child with anger issues but the next step we tend to take is to put them on medication knowing that the violence should have never transpired at least in their presence. When infants cry its because they are hungry or need changin' but a middle child cry witnessing his mother circumstance the anger manipulates his thinking patterns and causes the child to lash out uncontrollably even while in public.

And the parent who is trying her best to hide her encounter tends to pop the child or use force to try and get them to behave to avoid the stares and the murmurring of bystanders.

✦ ✦ ✦ ✦ ✦ ✦ ✦

* When a man dictates how much income she needs its called financial abuse if a man can't tend to his priorities such as paying their morgage or the up keep on their vehicles it once again becomes her fault while he tends to deal with it by having a strong drink and disrupting her peace I find it totally obnoxious for her to live day to day without having the authorities involve and saying no when ask if she wanna press charges and a good cop whose duty is to protect and serve should already know her signs of fear by the unlimited calls they have already dealt with throughout their 40 hours shift. A womans inclination when dealing with abuse is to protect the children and she will get frustrated enough to grab the kids and storm out with nothing but her pocketbook and no destination because she failed to plan.

---

* Ladies one time is one too many and the lie that it won't happen again is just that "A lie do not heed to it leave.

Most women have children of all ages but for her to manifest that her baggage weighs nothing is incredible. I'm going to make this statement and hopefully its coming from the wisest brain cell I have "The woman is the greatest enticement of the man we love your shape we lust over her curves and thickness we're captivated by a pretty smile and facial features and we constantly pursue you until we finally get you.

If you are a woman who prefer a man who doesn't drink or smoke keep your standards high and don't except anything other than that because those are not arguments waiting to transgress as someone of domestic violence they just have the notation since they don't smoke or drink they'll just remain flurtatious and a full committment isn't an option.

✦✦✦✦✦

* Lowering your standard is just increasing your vulnerability to sustain regrets. You ever watch a movie where the mother tell the daughter no you can't go to the party and she sneek out and go any way and while she out there she's snatched up and begging to wanna go home the

same place she left to seek adventure that's regret. Keep your standards high against our charming and conniving approaches. There are women who beared children for a man who whined up nothing like he partrayed to be and she getting older not even being recognize as a woman but a baby mama generations are becoming more unpredictable and the only thing that separate us is age difference. A woman has the ability to be more valuable as a mother, a sister or even a loyal friend but 90% of the time we chose to lust after her rather than get her best qualities. Make light of the situation if you will I'm all the brotherly love I need.

I can't allow myself to accumilate regrets as I focus on getting older I can't be relied on to make sure someone is bailed out I can't allow a empty room in my home to be occupied by some one who has no potential to ever come into their own I refuse to let my kindness be taken as a weakness. Men tend to lure women by having the finer things as if its being equally shared and we know the truth behind that for whatever reason you wanna play that game there are alot of board markers for you to choose from. Some people appear to be to needy and by judging their appearance they are overlooked and a great companion never get the chance to answer your prayer.

————————◆◆◆◆◆————————

* Because domestic violence is considered a taught behavior it has enlisted a great number of pupils who chose to carry the titles of criminal child abuse, aggravated assault, simple battery and a list of others which clearly says deception, mental illness, and evaluation the things that make his behavior patterns detrimental and unpredictable. To live in fear ladies is not a normal perception of living life.

When someone reach that level of anger to doust gas or lighter fluid on someone and then proceed to flick the lighter they are convince that you are worthless but whose really showing the characteristics of being unstable abusive people speak in abusive tones daily if he speaks to you or the kids in this manner "I said no, or where you going or where you been you could hear the aggression and its a clear sign of an abuser. I won't tell you, but their are ways to ask those questions. Of course the two of you have different taste for music but if his love of music clearly states that the woman is a bitch a hoe or any other degrating word to describe her he's fueling his temper for the next altercation.

---

* I titled this "When Her Baggage Weighed Nothing" watching my mother carry a 45 pound pocketbook around with everything in it except this book and I use to hate going to retrieve it when she ask for it. I want to address something encouraging to the young minds who also witnessing this act of violence you must remain focus this isn't just an act of calling the police this has to cleverly be planned out so that everyone can leave alive.

You have to be willing to turn down the bad behavior which you are learning to get a fair chance to be a productive citizen because you still have to live here. If you are questioning who side you should be taking don't second guess choose mama because when she's not facing the unnecessary she's the one that will hold you down you just have to do your part and control what you witness. Even when I was out there abusing drugs and alcohol I held my own I don't write books from doing research on the topics I write what I've experience. When looking for love she will bring around you who she felt was a good match and its risky because she's putting you in danger if it doesn't go well.

* * * * * * *

* I'll say this and I'll say it proudly not even I could walk the straight and narrow with the challenges life thrown in my path when I got tired of trying to jump every hurdle I simply started walking around them. Having to choose who you will live with

as divorce papers are filed for once think about your future and what will be best for you don't let the judge place you where you do not want to belong because later it will resurface. I could not walk out in public known how I really was but I did and some had the perception that I had a hard life and to a certain extent it was excepted but they had no clue I was a ticking time bomb because I kept everything bottled up and here I am now a author of 3 books with an outlet whenever my wagon seems full. Even though we share similarities we are different I just chose to march to the beat of my own drum "No one elses." You can't share your life experience with everyone cause everyone don't have your same interest.

———————— ✦✦✦✦✦ ————————

* Through all this the truth never left me but anger tried to destroy me. If you are a man and you stand on the principals of what's qualified to be considered a man you don't blakely call her derogatory names you respect the woman who bends

over backwards for you helping you pay off your probation, help you get from place to place, allow you to move in shortly after dating you, she takes you shopping and she gives you a key to come and go as you please and as soon as you realize you can't return the favor she becomes a fat bitch or a neighborhood hoe and the reason being because you had no intention from the jump to gain her support and back her up with the love she flatout wanted you are a deceiver and a deceiver can't be trusted because your intention doesn't care who you belittle. Which excuse gets you the most sympathy "I seen my daddy do it" or "My daddy was never in my life to show me how to treat a woman." I think its fair to say you are a living chance or you can become a silenced testimony and there's really no in between it really saddens me to have to write this because a few incidents could have been excused but here it is years later and the number of domestic violence toward the woman has increase dramatically.

* I am choosing to be in the sight of these aggressors because not enough "men" are protesting in their favor because this vindictive behavior has escalated throughout generations and because I had to witness this unprepared act of escaping I'm using my voice to address the fact and put a spin on things by letting you know where we stand "civilize lives matter". If you feel clenching your fist toward her helping you get your point across we will deal with you accordingly and hopefully the world will grasp the fact on what we won't tolerate.

Stop being force to smile in pictures when you know you're not happy.

This whole act of violence is about advantage and control and if you completely allow someone to strip you of your dignity what will you have left. "We can't forget the victims". Some will even go to the extent to threaten to kill you if you try to leave did you ever expect that from the man who showered you with flowers and gifts to win your heart instead of being told your a great mother and every man would dream of having you as a wife but instead you get told that your a sorry lazy ass worthless piece of shit and you have heard it so much 'til you don't even challenge it you simply embrace it as the truth. After watching statistics reach its highest peek just among young adults this is where we're at still trying to take the appropriate way of escaping with baggage that accumilated throughout the relationship.

<hr />

Stop lying to the ones that's asking are you o.k. or how has everything been going these predators are not unique. We see them throughout our daily routine either their seeking for a victim are trying to cover up what anger management couldn't fix. What I'm about to say I don't wanna hear it said no other way except how I said it, I'm not glorifying school and church shooting but they signified what untreated hurt and abuse can lead too. It wasn't the love of their parent alone that made them commit the act but the one who came into their life and turned it upside down and it clearly gave them the assumption if I'm gonna hurt then you're gonna hurt please read this carefully "When children are force to speak out from frustration its not gonna be said aloud on a public plat form its gonna be from what many failed to do and that's plan and plan is the keyword used to save lives as well as take lives I'm not a man confused about his lifestyle I abide by my marriage vows I keep a steady income I do 'alil bit more than I should when it comes to making sure a roof is over our head but what I'm mostly proud of I can seek help with anger if I feel my marriage is in danger. I wish I could have told my mother at that age that she never depreciate in value but since I didn't I'm now telling the mothers who are being treated in the most disrespectful manner that if a body is incarcerated so is his mind and since his time is from beginning to end he tells you what you wanna hear to take the ease off his bid. A sober mind thinks rational a intoxicated mind thinks wreckless. There are at least 25 different substances we have been introduced to that we feel to comfortable to part from blunts being the most recent. While its lit its doing what we've been told it'll do calm the nerves put you in a musical vibe but when you don't have it ladies how's the attitude an agitated person who has to have that blunt before the day comes to an end.

◆◆◆◆◆

Different grades bring about different circumstances if he's choosing street drugs you have the right to plan always have a fall back plan stop screaming on the inside feeling like no one hears you and the only way to be heard is to speak up and break your silence. Help me put these aggressors away under the law of reckless aggravated assault a minium of four years one has to be held responsible because this act is intentional stop allowing someone to make you the center of attention at your awaited funeral service reminiencing sharing memories of what you were like and I'm willing to bet it all one would say I had no idea or I didn't know just to keep guilt off of them.

------◆◆◆◆------

Whenever a woman is abuse sexually she shower and she vigiorously scrubbin' herself to feel cleanse once again leavin' her mental to become challenge and the thoughts are so rapidly happening that she has no time to process them and the out come can become detrimental to anyone not paying attention to notice her having flash backs or jokingly not taking her situation seriously and rightfully she isn't to blame knowing her attacker left her there and escape without her ever knowing who violated her. Growing up with a sister I learned to look at a woman within those guidelines and I also learned to go after what excites me romantically and my mother set the bar high if I ever needed to fulfill her absence those are the qualifications that I've lived by up to this point and I don't mix them because of their values. Truth is if I will fight my sister which I did growing up I also would show vulnerability and weakness in other areas when it come to her and I the bible calls it incest I call it "lusting" growing up I watch men eye balling the woman up and down as she walked by I've heard men say the most provoking thing as a catch line to get her attention skimpy clothes has never been o.k. it flat out intices the lustful eye of mankind we can go to a club and become one with our homeboy but we fail to look at her in a fatherly daughterly fashion or a mother and son all because of its up tempt habitat and the fuel it offers. What children are not understanding and I'm preferring to generations coming after me. The females who wore the black-eye whose ribs were fractured, who teeth was knockout, who was shot, burned, finger jammed crooked, deaf in one ear, sexually assaulted even poisoned she went above and beyond to keep you from being harmed and alot of you were not physically harmed but you were harmed by witnessing the act and yes you became baggage that she lugged and it weighed nothing to her. Some of you grew angry hearing about the slave trade and what happen to them as they tried to escape well her situation is no different the master is worst this time around its your dad or the man who she trusted to love and provide and protect the family. If you live with your mother and your not contributing around the house and getting into all kind of unnecessary trouble if she hasn't yelled at you in the highest pitched voice she has "You have no idea what I've been through to keep you safe consider yourself incapable of learning and may the rest of the world show you mercy. It saddens me because as I write this another domestic violence murder has taken place days before Christmas of 2020. This is how fast your life is being taken for granted and I'm learning... learning not to be so quick to ever say I tried to tell yall because I realize how difficult it is to escape alive. As an author I will continue to keep her memory alive and speak on my mom's behalf and as I stated earlier it never resignate in their mind that you belong to someone else besides them and yet gain I question God on why he's allowing this to turn mothers, sisters, aunts, girl friends, wives and our daughters world topsy turvy love should be the easiest of the spiritual needs to give but we see it isn't. Perhaps we should just catch on to what's blakely being said single parent mothers it has to just be you and the children no one else to bring an outsider definition of love into a home that has already been sustained. A man who isn't sure isn't always the answer and its definitely isn't worth the gamble. You now have to line your kids up in front of you with your back against the wall and see with a clear view who it is wanting to harm your family. Its books of this magnitude that has the funding power to sponsor single parents so that you don't jepardize your children humble well being and all children are humble but you can't just let unprecidented influences manipulate them. If you have been a single mother for sometime an surprisingly aggressive man surely isn't the answer raise them in your love in the same manner my mother whined up raising us. Facing her struggles alone until we grew up and she then proceeded her search. Times were much harder when my mother went through it and me logging down my insights should give you the manpower that's missing throughout homes nationwide to be able at anytime to pick up your baggage despite want it may weigh and find the peace that you rightfully deserve.

———————◆◆◆◆◆———————

I'll be the first to tell you its hard abiding within the guidelines of the spiritual man having to watch what you say and being liable for your actions because we face unprecedented hurdles on a daily basis which kick start ranting and negative behavior I would go as far as saying the woman deserves to be in a healthy spiritual filled relationship but don't be blinded or naive just to keep a man in your prescence. Spiritual growth can't be a one sided practice between you and your partner one can't go to counseling while the other stay home and watch the game with his homeboys. There are times when I forcefully have to cry out to our Lord and Savior for the well being of my wife and that's natural because I'm not asking to prevent from harming my wife I'm asking for assurance.

✦✦✦✦✦

If you are within a relationship and you have to walk on eggshells that is the sign of an unhealthy house hold. It was said by those of great knowledge girls mature faster than boys and I do find that statement to be truthful because a female can produce a newborn and her whole life is to nurture when a male live off instinct and he's convince by the appearance of facial hair and his physique but the mind has yet to catch up and the values in which he was brought up are not a priority let alone practice.

But for some reason it always seems to me if you play devil advocate or tamper with evil you will get a quicker result than when you pray and receive your blessing. Take a moment and ask yourself which one do domestic violence fall under? Being submissive or dominate control its a fact that a woman can and have abuse men but I do not have the desire to elaborate or give any justification because of how it was exercised to me even though the woman came across the garden's brainish creature and gotten us banished from paradise I still married with the hope of putting her hand into my hand and taking our first stride into a hard life together because she is his very own creation and she is of me a rib in which no other religion cared to use and so I chose to humble myself and not create an act of self-infliction.

Even in the heat of things a man should be able to walk away or leave and have a cool down period if it proceed to get that worst. I am not in the business of convincing I titled this "When Her Baggage Weighed Nothing" to help regain your hope that deliberately changed your life without warning. It furture surprises me that not one man who have committed the act of domestic violence took the ignitiontive to shine light on why they must get excessively physical with a woman instead we allow our daughters to receive the message through the artist, the song, the youtube video this act of violence flatout tells me that if you are not happy and content with a full grown adult you will stoop as low as to manipulate a younger person more enticing to the eye. Let's use a vase for example everything that gets broken is not considered a loss if you kneel down and gather the main pieces you can piece the vase back into a whole and the next one to lay eyes on it value it as an antique and its placed on the mantle out of reach so that it won't get shattered and lose complete value. If the son see the daddy being abusive its a proven fact he will become abusive only this time its felony child endangerment and humanly wounds never get a chance to heal after all that I've been through the alcohol abuse the over excessive usage of self medicating not to mention the enforced hand of the court I can proudly say that I am delighted to have dropped out of that race. If a man is refusing to allow a woman to embrace him in a loving manner and he's refuses to nurture her effort follow my gut feeling and let it go.

------◆◆◆◆◆------

If things are fine one minute and all hell breaking loose the next its clearly an act of inticipation build-up sorry that the hearts of men are not put into a glass case with the inscription briefly telling about the person and ladies you always has to remember what it took for you to get the individual is what you have to do to keep 'em. A man would rather remain single or just keep the relationship steady if he knew you wasn't gonna be sexually active throughout the ordeal the two bodies are different and when he's aroused and your not and your tired and don't feel up to it you just sent a hue of negative impulsives into his brain because he has a urge that needed to be met. If this is the case with you don't hold on to that person for what they can do for you in other areas its best to find the common ground and let go apparently there's a great misunderstanding when it comes to confinement and committment and it seems that committment is the trickery to endure you into confinement and I'm talking about the confinement in which you can't move around freely.

A certain percentage of us we try to remain humane throughout a great portion of our lives and the other percentage of us we have problems and habits that we should of have had broken at an early age and now they are starting to resurface and by self medicating they are becoming uncontrollable unpredictable and charges are accumililating putting you and yours in grave danger.

✦✦✦✦✦

Every young adult has heard and excepted the fact that weed is from the earth street drugs exspecially weed isn't the prescribe drug to cope with PTSD its not the miracle drug to cope with schizophrenia its not the drug that will pamper being bipolar. Each one of these mental illnesses has a medication to stabilize ones way of thinking but the regular usage of marijunia keep the charges adding up and domestic violence becomes the next day news headline.

Printed in the United States
by Baker & Taylor Publisher Services